Meet the Chara

Asalamu Alaikum!
My Name is Arwa!

Peace be with you!
My name is Mustafa!

Mustafa and Arwa Adventure Series

ISBN-13: 978-0692666678
ISBN-10: 0692666672

for Lujain

MUSTAFA AND ARWA GO ON A WUDU ADVENTURE

By: Mekram Mohammad

MUSLIM
PILLARS

Time to pray, let's make wudu!

Don't you worry, it's
easy to do!

Say Bismillah before
you start.

Say it out loud, and in your heart!

Wash your hands, your fingers,
and in between.

Wash them around until you're sparkling clean!

Rinse your mouth and swish it out.

Making sure you're clean is
what it's all about

Time to rinse that cute little nose.

Let me hear those short little blows!

Splash your face from your forehead to your chin.

It's so fun, it'll make you grin!

Wipe your arms, from your
elbows to your wrist.

Just make sure, no parts missed!

Wet your head with a ruba-dub-dub.

Get those ears with a
final scrub!

Sink those feet in as far as it goes.

Don't you dare miss those toes!

Now you're ready to go and pray.

Meeting Allah five times a day!

Wudu Glossary

- The Prophet, peace be upon him, said "**cleanliness** is half of faith".

- Wudu is the ritual washing performed by Muslims **before prayer**.

- Muslims must be **clean** and wear good clothes before they present themselves before God.

- If there is no water present, **Tayammum** is performed, which is doing a variation of wudu with sand/dust.

The End!

Join us on our next adventure Insha'Allah!

facebook.com/muslimpillars

instagram.com/muslimpillars

CHECK OUT OUR OTHER TITLES!

AVAILABLE ON AMAZON.COM & MUSLIMPILLARS.COM

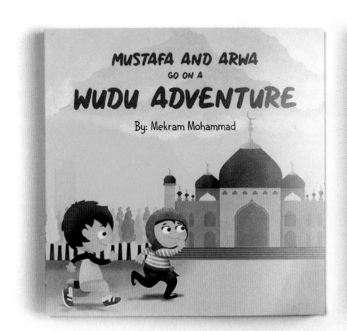

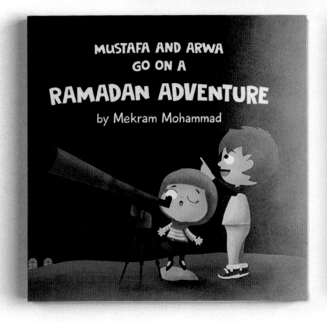

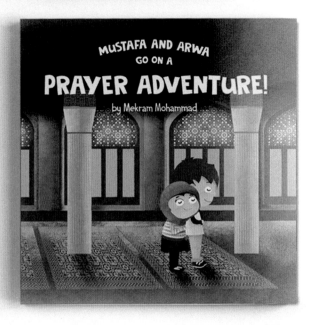

Made in the USA
Middletown, DE
31 July 2020